UKULELE

Disney
FROZEN II

MUSIC FROM THE MOTION PICTURE SOUNDTRACK

ISBN 978-1-5400-8371-5

HAL•LEONARD®

Visit Hal Leonard Online at
www.halleonard.com

Contact us:
Hal Leonard
7777 West Bluemound Road
Milwaukee, WI 53213
Email: info@halleonard.com

In Europe, contact:
Hal Leonard Europe Limited
42 Wigmore Street
Marylebone, London, W1U 2RN
Email: info@halleonardeurope.com

In Australia, contact:
Hal Leonard Australia Pty. Ltd.
4 Lentara Court
Cheltenham, Victoria, 3192 Australia
Email: info@halleonard.com.au

Contents

All Is Found

Music and Lyrics by Kristen Anderson-Lopez and Robert Lopez

Some Things Never Change

Music and Lyrics by Kristen Anderson-Lopez and Robert Lopez

like the feel of your hand — in mine. — Some things stay the same, —

like how we get a - long — just fine. — Like an old — stone wall — that -'ll nev - er fall, —

OLAF: like how we get a - long — just fine. —

Straight 16ths

some things are al - ways true! _____ Some things nev - er — change, —

___ like how I'm hold-ing on tight — to you. **KRISTOFF:** 2. The

leaves are al - read-y fall - ing. Sven, it feels like the fu-ture is call - ing! **SVEN:** Are you

tell-ing me to-night you're gon-na get down on — one knee? _____ **KRISTOFF:**
Yeah, but I'm

really bad at planning these things — out, like candle-light and pulling of rings — out.

SVEN: Maybe you should leave all the romantic stuff — to me.

KRISTOFF: Yeah,

Chorus
Swing 16ths

some things never change, _ like the love that I feel — for her. _ Some things stay the same, _

like how reindeers are eas - i - er. But if I _____ commit _____ and I go for it, _____ I'll

know what to say and do! Right? **SVEN:** Some things nev - er ____ change. ____

KRISTOFF:
____ Sven, the pres-sure is all ____ on you.

Bridge

Am   B♭   Am

ELSA: The winds are rest-less; could that be why I'm hear-ing this call? Is some-thing com-ing? I'm

B♭   F   C

not sure I want things to change ___ at all. These days are pre-cious, can't

Dm   Am   G

let them slip a-way... ___ I can't freeze this mo-ment, but

B♭   **Interlude**   F C B♭

I can still go out ___ and seize this ___ day!! ___

F C B♭   F C B♭   C   D

ARENDELLE: Ah, ___ oh. ___ 3. The

Verse
Straight 16ths

G   D   C   G   D   C

wind blows a lit-tle bit cold - er.   **OLAF:** And you all look a lit-tle bit old - er!   **ANNA:** It's

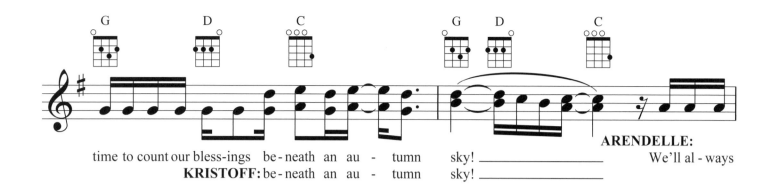

time to count our bless-ings be-neath an au - tumn sky! _____ **ARENDELLE:** We'll al - ways
KRISTOFF: be-neath an au - tumn sky! _____

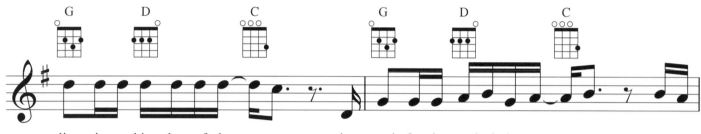

live in a king-dom of plen - ty that stands for the good of the man - y! **ELSA:** And I

prom-ise you the flag of Ar - en-delle will al - ways fly!! **ANNA:** Our flag will al - ways

fly!
ARENDELLE: Our flag will al - ways, our flag will al - ways fly!

Chorus

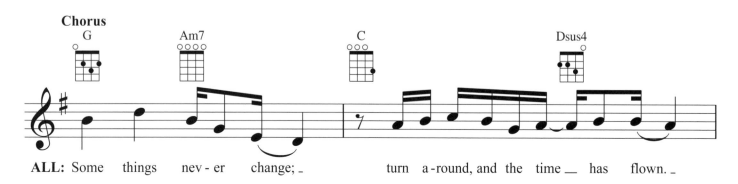

ALL: Some things nev - er change; _ turn a-round, and the time _ has flown. _

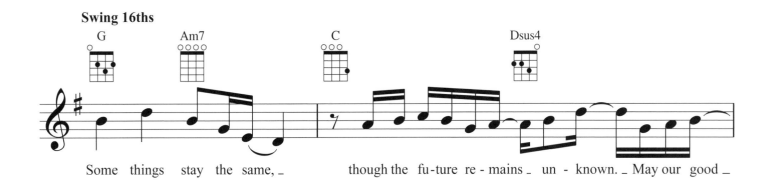

Some things stay the same, _ though the fu-ture re-mains _ un - known. _ May our good _

_ luck last, _ may our past _ be past. _ Time's mov-ing fast, it's true! _

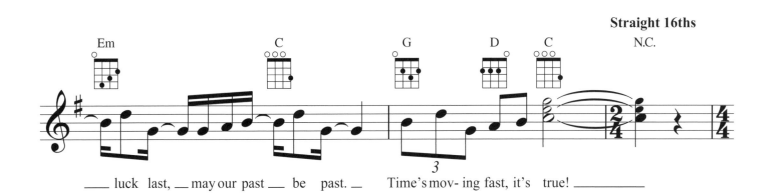

ELSA, OLAF & KRISTOFF:
Some things nev - er ___ change... ___
ANNA: Some things nev - er ___ change, ___ and I'm hold-ing on tight _ to

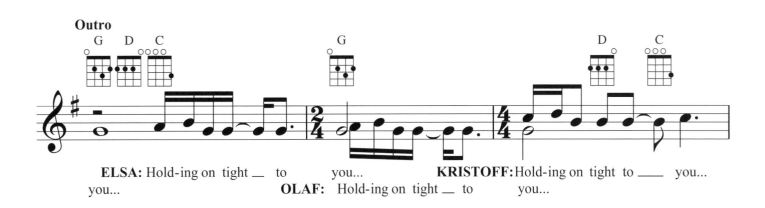

ELSA: Hold-ing on tight _ to you... **KRISTOFF:** Hold-ing on tight to ___ you...
you... **OLAF:** Hold-ing on tight _ to you...

ANNA: I'm hold-ing on tight _ to you.

Into the Unknown

Music and Lyrics by Kristen Anderson-Lopez and Robert Lopez

Recorded a half step higher.

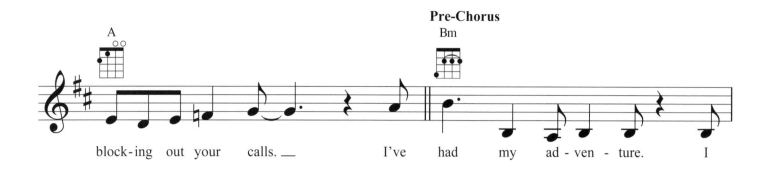

A

blocking out your calls. ___ I've had my ad-ven-ture.   I

Pre-Chorus
Bm

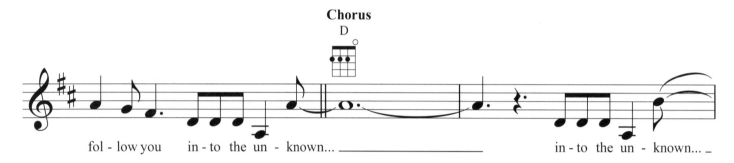

Gmaj7

don't need some-thing new! ___ I'm a-fraid of what I'm risk-ing if I

Chorus
D

fol-low you in-to the un-known... _____   in-to the un-known... _

G   Bm

_____   in-to the un-known! _____

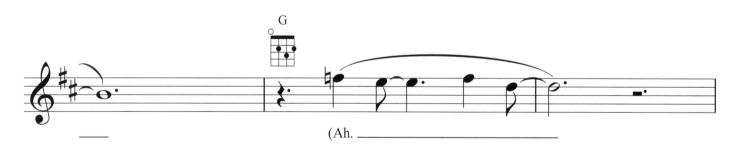

G

___   (Ah. _____

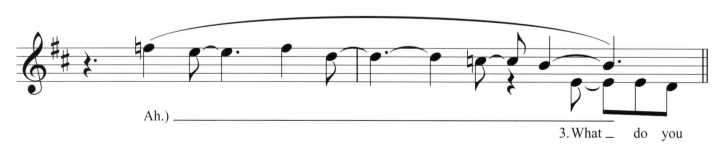

Ah.) _____

3. What _ do you

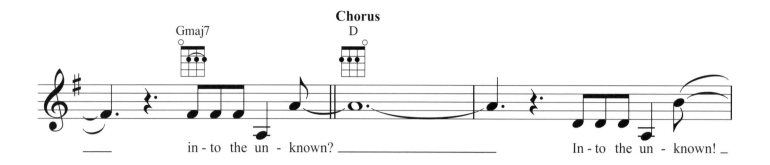

in - to the un - known? _____ In - to the un - known! _

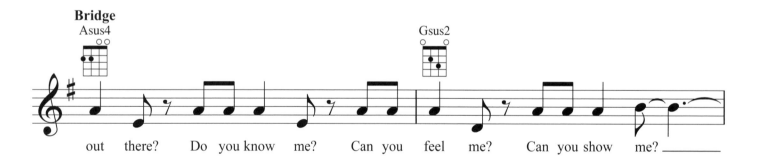

_____ In - to the un - known! _____

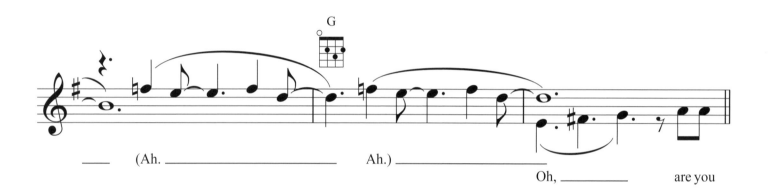

___ (Ah. _____ Ah.) _____ Oh, _____ are you

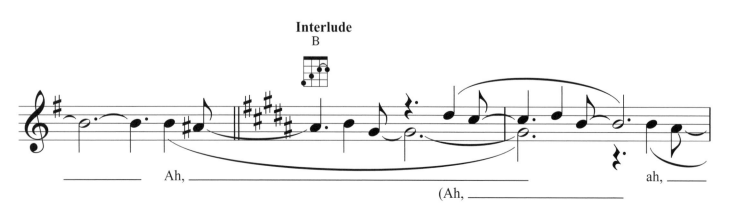

out there? Do you know me? Can you feel me? Can you show me? _____

Ah, _____ ah,
(Ah, _____

ah,   ah,   ah,

ah,   ah,   ah,

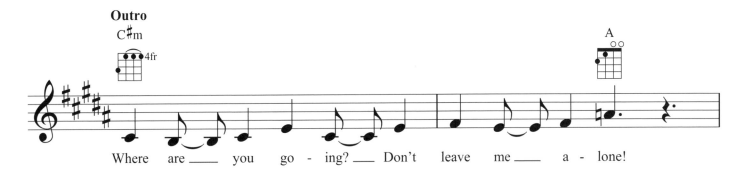

ah,   ah.

ah,   ah.)

Outro

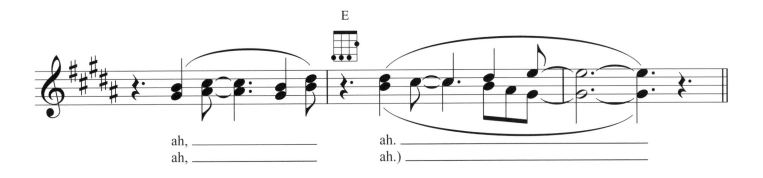

Where are   you go - ing?   Don't leave me   a - lone!

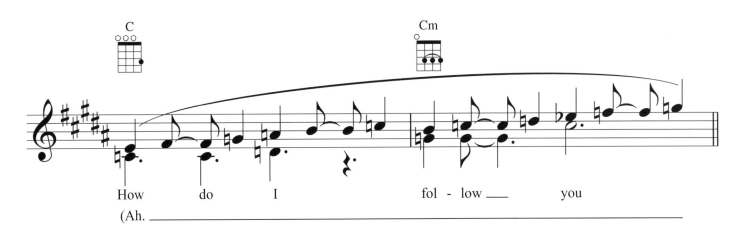

How do I   fol - low   you

(Ah.

Dramatically

in - to the   un - known?

Ah.)

When I Am Older

Music and Lyrics by Kristen Anderson-Lopez and Robert Lopez

OLAF: 1. This will all make sense when I am old - er.

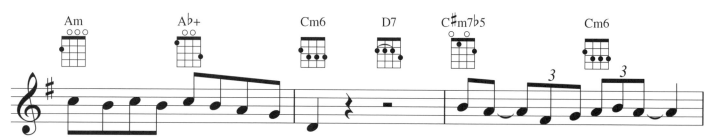

Some - day, I will see that this makes sense. One day, ___ when I'm old and wise, ___

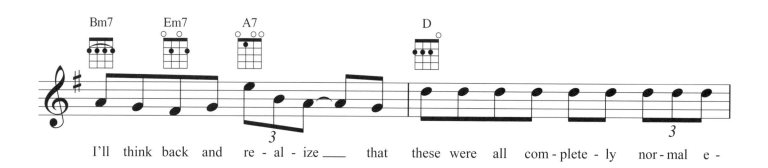

I'll think back and re - al - ize ___ that these were all com - plete - ly nor - mal e -

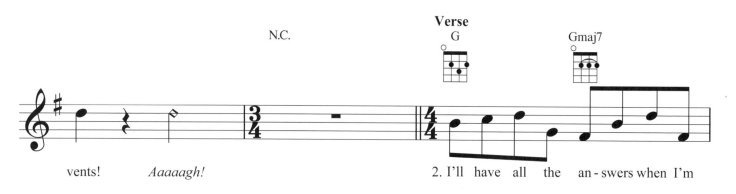

vents! *Aaaaagh!* 2. I'll have all the an - swers when I'm

* Recorded a half step higher.

old - er! Like, why we're in this dark, en - chant - ed wood.

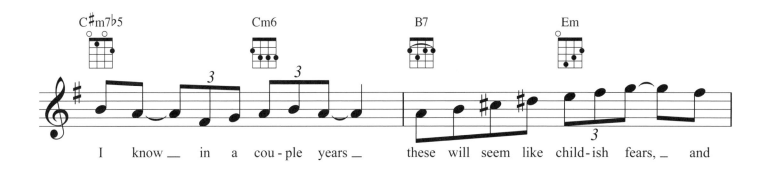

I know __ in a cou - ple years __ these will seem like child - ish fears, __ and

so I know this is - n't bad, it's good! *(Spoken:)* Excuse me.

Bridge

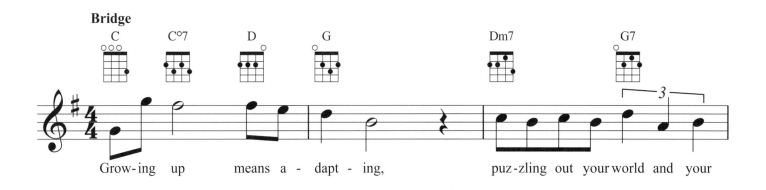

Grow - ing up means a - dapt - ing, puz - zling out your world and your

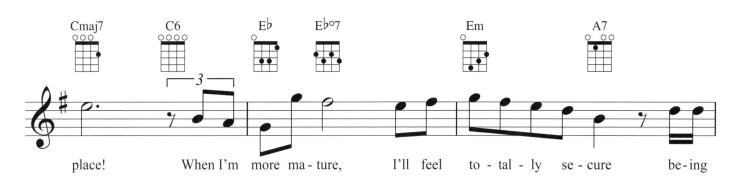

place! When I'm more ma - ture, I'll feel to - tal - ly se - cure be - ing

watched by some-thing ___ with a creep-y, creep-y face. ___ AAAH!!!! AAAH!!!!

Outro-Verse

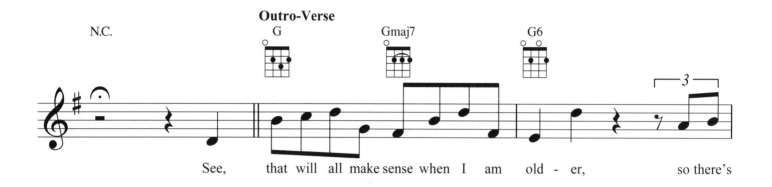

See, that will all make sense when I am old - er, so there's

Slower (♩♩ = ♩♩)

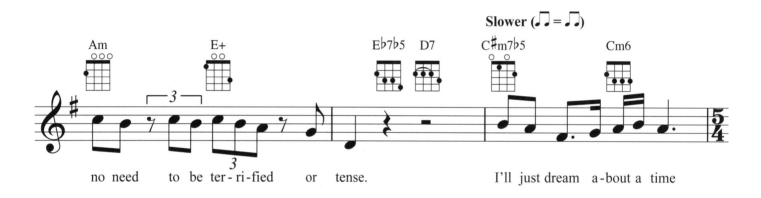

no need to be ter - ri-fied or tense. I'll just dream a-bout a time

Tempo I (♩♩ = ♩ ♪)

when I'm in my a - ged prime. 'Cause when you're old - er,

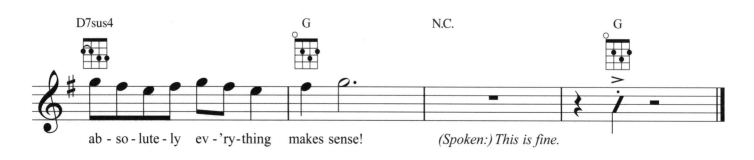

ab - so - lute - ly ev - 'ry-thing makes sense! *(Spoken:) This is fine.*

Reindeers(s) Are
Better Than People (Cont.)

Music and Lyrics by Kristen Anderson-Lopez and Robert Lopez

First note

Slowly, freely

N.C.

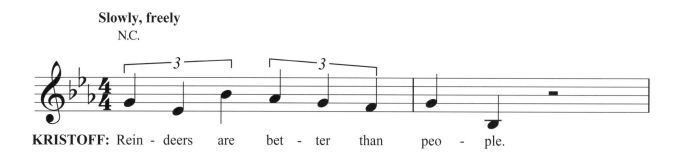

KRISTOFF: Rein - deers are bet - ter than peo - ple.

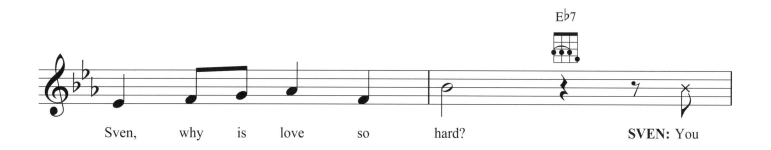

Sven, why is love so hard? **SVEN:** You

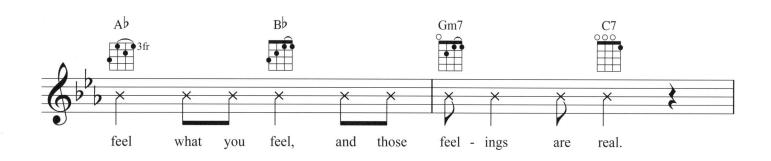

feel what you feel, and those feel - ings are real.

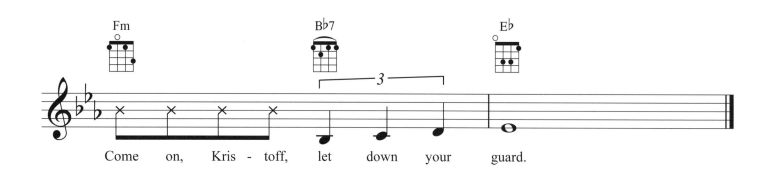

Come on, Kris - toff, let down your guard.

24

Lost in the Woods

Music and Lyrics by Kristen Anderson-Lopez and Robert Lopez

Verse
Moderately, in 2

KRISTOFF: 1. A - gain you're gone, ___ off on a

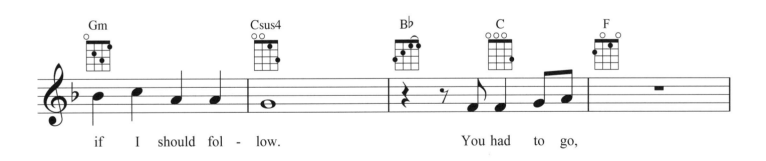

dif - f'rent path ___ than mine. ___ I'm left be - hind, ___ won - der - ing

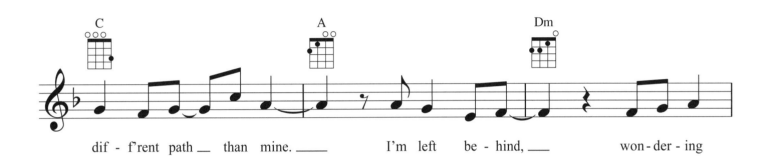

if I should fol - low. You had to go,

and, of course, it's al - ways fine. ___ I

Recorded a minor 3rd higher.

prob - 'ly could catch up with you to - mor - row. _____ But is

Pre-Chorus

this what it feels _____ like to be grow - ing a - part? _

_____ When did I be - come the one _____ who's al - ways

Chorus

chas - ing your heart? _____ Now I turn a - round_ and find

I am lost in the woods. _____ North is south,

right is left when you're _ gone. _____ I'm the one _

who sees you home, but now I'm lost in the woods,

and I don't know what path you are on.

I'm lost in the woods.

Verse

2. Up 'til now, the next step was a

ques - tion of how; _____ I nev - er thought it was a

ques - tion of wheth - er. Who am I _____

if I'm not your guy? _____ Where am

I if we're not to - geth - er for - ev -

Chorus

- er? _____ Now I know you're my true North,

'cause I am lost in the woods. _____ Up is down, _

_____ day is night when you're not _____ there. _____ Oh, _____

you're my on - ly land - mark, so I'm lost in the woods, _____

won - der - ing if you still care.   But I'll wait

Outro

_ for a sign _ that I'm _ your _

_ path, 'cause you _ are mine.   Un - til

then, I'm lost in the woods. _

_ I'm lost in the woods. _

I'm lost in _ the woods.

Show Yourself

Music and Lyrics by Kristen Anderson-Lopez and Robert Lopez

Verse
Moderately

ELSA: 1. Ev - 'ry inch of me is trem - bling, but not from the

cold. _____ Some - thing is fa - mil - iar, like a dream I can

reach but not ___ quite ___ hold. ___ I can sense you there, _

like a friend I've al - ways known. _____ I'm ar -

riv - ing, and it feels like I am home. _____ I have

Recorded a half step lower.

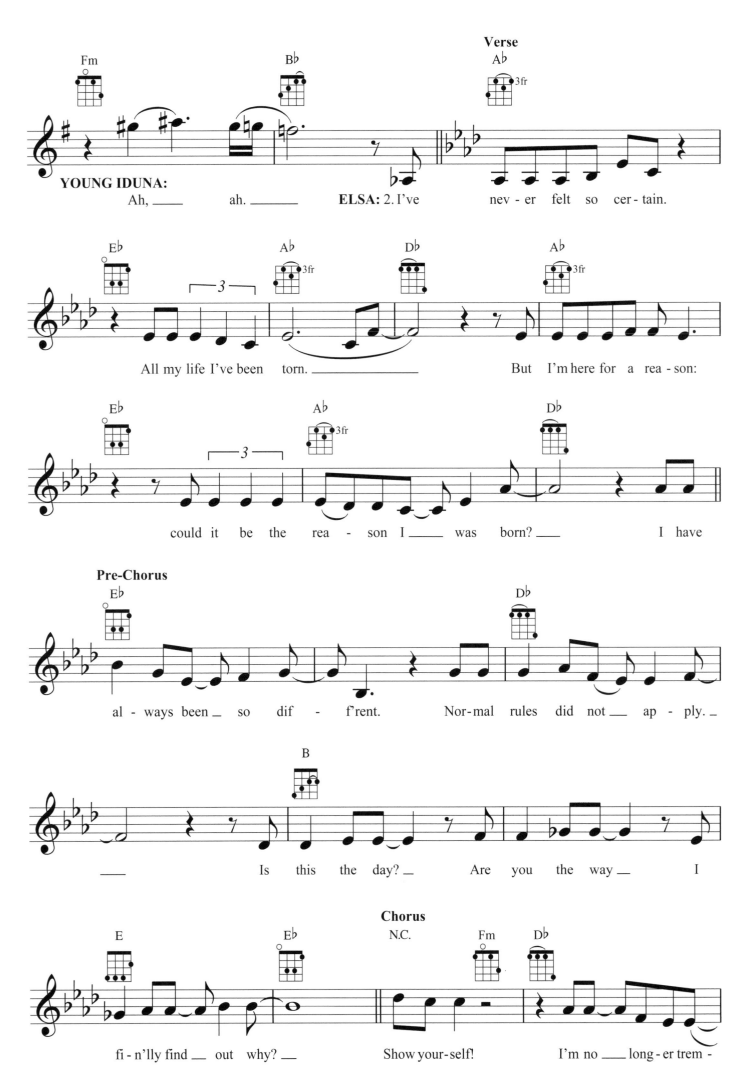

-bling! Here I ____ am: ____ I've __ come so __

__ far! __ You are the an - swer I've wait - ed for all of my __

__ life! _____ Oh, show your - self: _____

__ let me see who you are. _____

Bridge

Come to __ me __ now. O - pen __ your _ door.

Don't make __ me __ wait one mo - ment more! Oh, __

come to _____ me now. _____ O - pen ____ your

door. _____ Don't make ___ me ___ wait one mo - ment

more! _____

Interlude
Slowly, majestically

CHORUS: (Where the North - wind _____ meets the sea, there's a

riv - er _____ full of mem - o - ry.) _____ **IDUNA:** Come, my dar - ling, home - ward ____

Chorus
Moderately, as before

____ bound. ___ **ELSA:** I am found! **ELSA/IDUNA:** Show your - self! ____

34

The Next Right Thing

Music and Lyrics by Kristen Anderson-Lopez and Robert Lopez

* Recorded a half step higher.

_____ blind - ly toward the light, and do the next right

thing.

Outro

And with the dawn, what comes

then when it's clear that ev - 'ry- thing will nev - er be the

same a - gain? _____ Then I'll

With freedom

make the choice to hear that voice, and

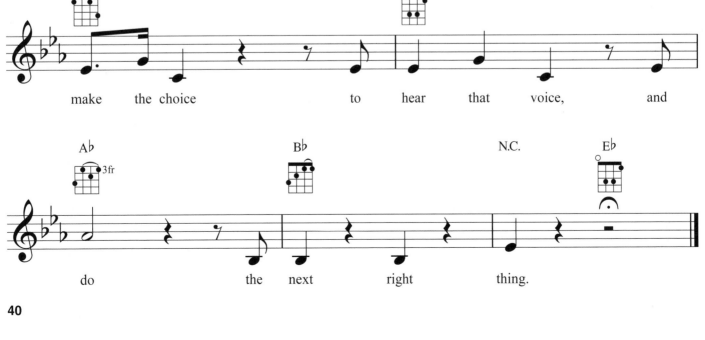

do the next right thing.